S0-ARY-055

MAPPING

PEOPLE

BY
MADELINE TYLER

Published in 2020 by KidHaven Publishing, an imprint of Greenhaven Publishing, LLC
353 3rd Avenue, Suite 255, New York, NY 10010

© 2020 Booklife Publishing

This edition is published by arrangement with Booklife Publishing.

All rights reserved. No part of this book may be reproduced in any
form without permission in writing from the publisher, except by a reviewer.

Written by: Madeline Tyler
Edited by: Kirsty Holmes
Designed by: Drue Rintoul

Cataloging-in-Publication Data

Names: Tyler, Madeline.
Title: Mapping people / Madeline Tyler.
Description: New York : KidHaven Publishing, 2020. | Series: Maps and mapping | Includes glossary and index.
Identifiers: ISBN 9781534531116 (pbk.) | ISBN 9781534530225 (library bound) | ISBN 9781534531529 (6 pack) | ISBN 9781534531055 (ebook)
Subjects: LCSH: Human geography--Juvenile literature. | Population--Juvenile literature. | Maps--Juvenile literature.
| Map reading--Juvenile literature.
Classification: LCC GF48.T95 2020 | DDC 300.22'3--dc23

Image Credits
All images are courtesy of Shutterstock.com, unless otherwise specified. With thanks to Getty Images, Thinkstock Photo and iStockphoto.
Front Cover – Dmitry Polonskiy, Rusla Ruseyn. 2 – ESB Professional. 4&5 – Rawpixel.com, Rainer Lesniewski, D1min, Andrey_Popov. 6&7 – hobbit, Denis Cristo, By PawelS (Own work) [CC BY-SA 3.0 (https://creativecommons.org/licenses/by-sa/3.0)], via Wikimedia Commons, Hilch. 8&9 – blvdon, City Escapes Nature Photo, vinap. 10&11 – Sudowoodo. 12&13 – SUSAN LEGGETT. 14&15 – Zurijeta, Lora Sutyagina, By Adityamadhav83 (Own work) [CC BY-SA 3.0 (https://creativecommons.org/licenses/by-sa/3.0)], via Wikimedia Commons. 16&17 – George Dolgikh, dramaj, i_sedano, Luchenko Yana. 18&19 – By Viajes_de_colon.svg: Phirosiberia derivative work: Phirosiberia (Viajes_de_colon.svg) [CC BY-SA 3.0 (https://creativecommons.org/licenses/by-sa/3.0) or GFDL (http://www.gnu.org/copyleft/fdl.html)], via Wikimedia Commons, By Jon Platek. Blank map by en:User:Reisio. [CC BY-SA 3.0 (https://creativecommons.org/licenses/by-sa/3.0) or GFDL (http://www.gnu.org/copyleft/fdl.html)], via Wikimedia Commons. 20&21 – mr.Timmi, Claudio Divizia. 22&23 – Rainer Lesniewski, By Eric Gaba (Sting – fr:Sting) [GFDL (http://www.gnu.org/copyleft/fdl.html), CC-BY-SA-3.0 (http://creativecommons.org/licenses/by-sa/3.0/) or CC BY-SA 2.5 (https://creativecommons.org/licenses/by-sa/2.5)], via Wikimedia Commons, By User:Andrein, with the assistance of EraNavigator (Own work) [CC BY-SA 3.0 (https://creativecommons.org/licenses/by-sa/3.0) or GFDL (http://www.gnu.org/copyleft/fdl.html)], via Wikimedia Commons, ekler. 24&25 – shooarts, tatishdesign, Allexxandar, By Mouser (Own work) [GFDL (http://www.gnu.org/copyleft/fdl.html) or CC-BY-SA-3.0 (http://creativecommons.org/licenses/by-sa/3.0/)], via Wikimedia Commons. 26&27 – Roman Pyshchyk, Rob Wilson, M-SUR, By Carport [CC BY-SA 3.0 (https://creativecommons.org/licenses/by-sa/3.0)], via Wikimedia Commons, Dr Morley Read. 28&29 – Randy Miramontez, Wachiwit, Patricia Hofmeester, Gervasio S. _ Eureka_89, NEstudio, Lasse Hendriks. 30 – george studio, Fotografiche.

Printed in the United States of America

CPSIA compliance information: Batch #BS19KL: For further information contact Greenhaven Publishing LLC, New York, New York at 1-844-317-7404

CONTENTS

Words that look like **this** are explained in the glossary on page 31.

What Is a Map?

Maps are **diagrams** that show parts of the world and how they are connected. Maps can show a big area, like the entire world, or a small area, like a village or woodland. Some maps only show natural **features** of the landscape, like mountains and rivers. Other maps show where buildings and roads are. Some maps only show specific things, like amusement park maps, which are for visitors to find their way around the park and plan their day.

FUN PASS AMUSEMENT PARK

With this map, a visitor can see where all the rides and roller coasters are and how to get to each one.

BY NOT INCLUDING OTHER INFORMATION, THE MAP OF AFRICA IS EASIER TO READ.

CHOOSING WHAT TO MAP

A mapmaker, called a cartographer, often can't put all parts of an area on a map. Because some things are left out, or simplified, a map doesn't always look exactly like a place. It is a drawing instead of a photo. Maps are useful to see certain features, **landmarks**, people, vegetation, or animals. The finished map can show some of these things clearly, but can't show everything, so they have to choose what is important.

This map of Africa only shows some natural features, like vegetation, and not towns or cities.

GEOGRAPHIC MAPS

There are different maps for different purposes. Some are: road or street maps for planning journeys; climatic maps that show typical weather of a region depending on the season; weather maps, which let people know what the weather will be like in the near future – such as today or tomorrow; political maps that highlight the size of countries and where the borders are; and terrain maps, which trace the ups and downs of the land.

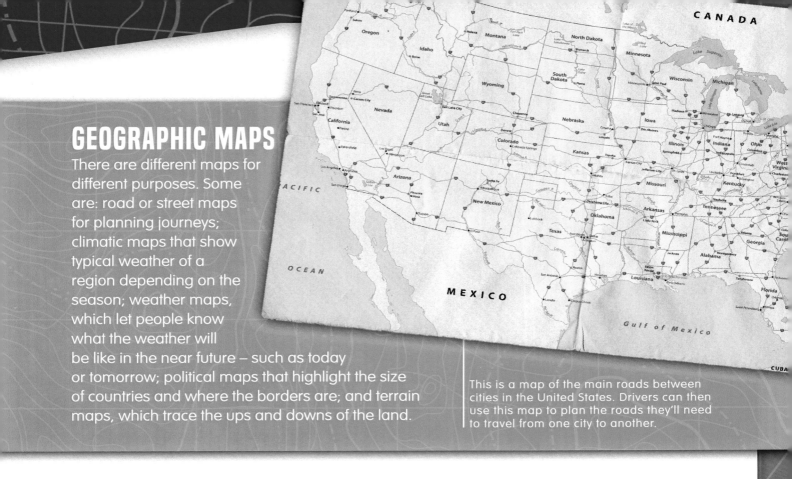

This is a map of the main roads between cities in the United States. Drivers can then use this map to plan the roads they'll need to travel from one city to another.

Non-Geographic Maps

There are even maps of objects and other things that aren't on the surface of the Earth. There are maps of space, such as solar system maps. There are tree maps that show the order that things happened and how they are linked. For example, a family tree is an easy way to see how everyone in a family is related. Mind maps are ways to come up with ideas that are linked to one main topic.

This is a map of our solar system.

Different topics can be drawn as mind maps.

MAPPING PEOPLE

Maps are a very useful tool and have been used by people for thousands of years. They are often used for **navigation** or for showing the locations of different countries and cities, but they are also helpful for plotting landmarks and displaying information. It is even possible to map people. This is part of a topic called human geography. Maps can be used to show lots of information about people, including how many people live in a specific place, how far they may have traveled to get there, and what languages they speak.

Maps are like pictures, and can be **color coded** to show the data in a simple way. Sometimes it is quicker and easier to read information from a map than it is from a graph or spreadsheet.

Not all maps look the same or show the same types of information. Two types of maps that are used to map people are cartograms and choropleth maps.

CARTOGRAMS

Geographical, or **topographical**, maps focus on the physical world and are usually geographically accurate, meaning that what you see on a map looks more or less like it does in the real world. They show natural features like mountains, oceans, and rivers. Political maps are similar to topographical maps, but instead they focus on countries, borders, and cities, and where these things actually are.

Cartograms are very different and are not geographically accurate. They show information like population numbers, the ages of citizens, or the amount of money a country has. Places on the map are made bigger or smaller depending on this information.

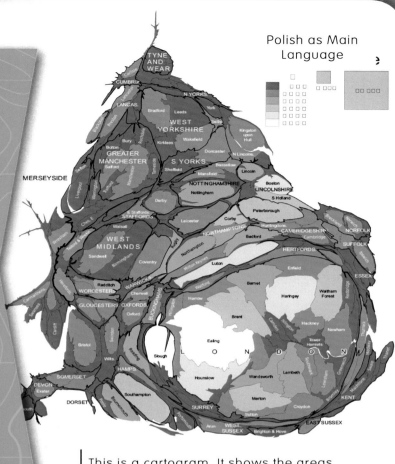

Polish as Main Language

This is a cartogram. It shows the areas in Great Britain where lots of people speak Polish as their main language.

Choropleths

Choropleth maps are similar to cartograms. They show information about people, like life expectancy or population density (see page 8). Instead of making the countries or regions different sizes, they are colored in different colors or shades. Every choropleth is different, but usually the scale goes from a light shade to a dark shade. Cartograms are also sometimes colored in this way.

This is an example of a choropleth map. It shows the population density around the world.

World Human Population
Persons/sq km

- >500
- 100-500
- 10-100
- <10

POPULATION

What Is Population Density?

In some parts of the world, there are lots of people living very close to each other. In other areas, there are very few people and they may live very far away from each other. Population density can be used to measure how populated an area is. Population density is the average number of people who live in an area. It is a way of measuring population **distribution** and is usually measured in people per square mile or kilometer.

Cities like New York in the U.S. are densely populated, meaning a lot of people live there, close together. Rural places are very sparsely populated, meaning few people live there, and they live farther apart.

NEW YORK CITY IS ONE OF THE MOST DENSELY POPULATED CITIES IN THE U.S. THERE ARE OVER 10,000 PEOLE PER 0.4 SQUARE MILE (1 SQ KM).

GREENLAND IS THE LEAST DENSELY POPULATED **TERRITORY** IN THE WORLD. THERE ARE ONLY 0.03 PEOPLE PER 0.4 SQUARE MILE (1 SQ KM) – AROUND ONE PERSON PER 20.5 SQUARE MILES (33 SQ KM).

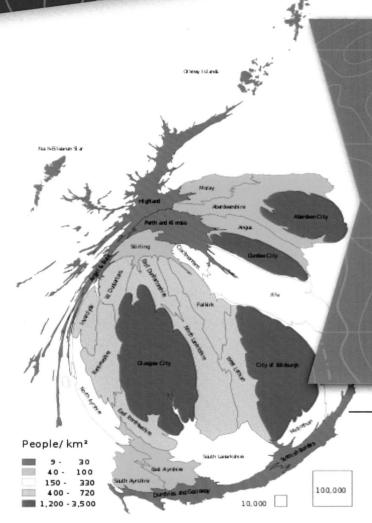

People/ km²

- 9 - 30
- 40 - 100
- 150 - 330
- 400 - 720
- 1,200 - 3,500

10,000   100,000

To calculate the population density of a country or area, you must first know the population. One method of calculating the population of a country is through a census. A census is a survey that everyone in the country must complete. It asks questions about where you live, where you were born, what your main language is, and what your religion is.

A census is taken every ten years in the U.S. This allows the government and **statisticians** to make new calculations on the country's population.

This cartogram shows population numbers in Scotland. It looks very different from a topographical or political map of Scotland.

Mapping Population Density

Once the data from the census has been collected, the population density can be calculated. This can then be displayed on a cartogram or a choropleth map.

It is important to know how many people live somewhere. The government can use this information to make sure there are enough hospitals, schools, trains, and buses for everyone.

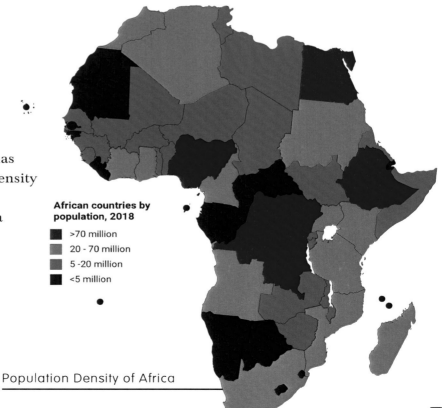

African countries by population, 2018

- >70 million
- 20 - 70 million
- 5 -20 million
- <5 million

Population Density of Africa

STATS ON MAPS

Maps can show more than population numbers and densities. They can show where different languages are spoken, what sports are popular around the world, and even what the average life expectancy is in different countries.

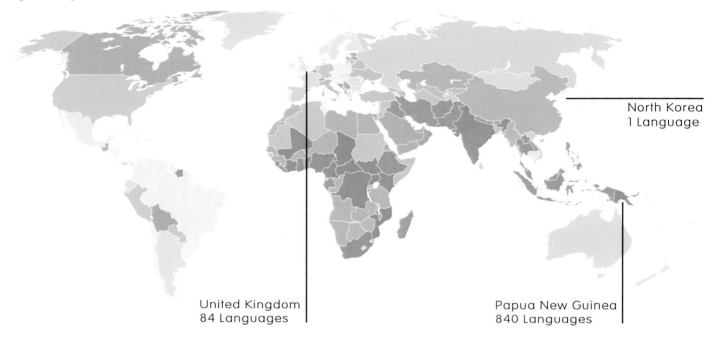

North Korea
1 Language

United Kingdom
84 Languages

Papua New Guinea
840 Languages

In many countries, the people who live there speak more than one language. These languages are sometimes different from the languages that their friends and neighbors speak. This map shows which countries have the highest **diversity** of languages.

LANGUAGES OF SOUTH AMERICA

Although the citizens of a country may speak hundreds of different languages, most countries have at least one language that they recognize as their official language. The official language is usually the language that is spoken within the government of the country. Bolivia has 39 official languages – one of the highest numbers of official languages in the world.

Spanish

Portuguese

English

French

Dutch

Spanish & Guarani

Spanish & Native Languages

38 OUT OF THE 39 OFFICIAL LANGUAGES OF BOLIVIA ARE NATIVE LANGUAGES.

This choropleth map of South America shows the different languages spoken across the continent. Can you count how many countries speak each language?

SPORTS

Different sports are popular in different countries, and even in different U.S. states. American football is the favorite sport amongst the majority of U.S. states, while most of South America prefers soccer, which is called football.

CAN YOU SEE YOUR FAVORITE SPORT ON THE MAP? WHERE WOULD YOU LIVE IN THE AMERICAS BASED ON YOUR FAVORITE SPORT?

Soccer/Football

Baseball

Cricket

Ice Hockey

American Football

LIFE EXPECTANCY

Not everyone in the world will live for the same length of time. Some people might live for nearly 100 years, while in other places, people can expect to live to around age 60. Life expectancy is how long a person is predicted to live for. This can change depending on what country you live in and how you live your life. War, **famine**, and **drought** can all reduce a person's life expectancy, while a healthy lifestyle, education, and access to good health care can increase life expectancy.

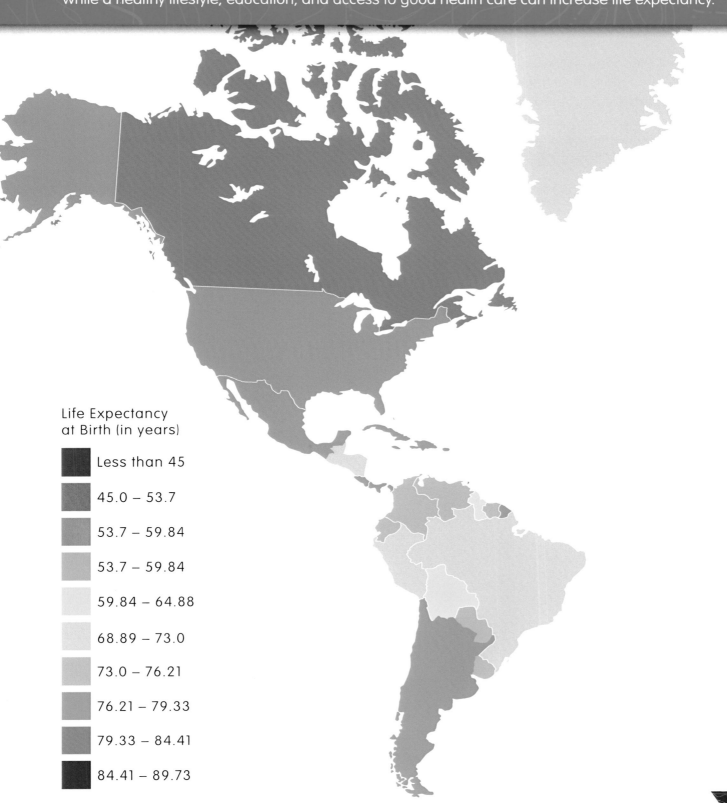

Life Expectancy at Birth (in years)

- Less than 45
- 45.0 – 53.7
- 53.7 – 59.84
- 53.7 – 59.84
- 59.84 – 64.88
- 68.89 – 73.0
- 73.0 – 76.21
- 76.21 – 79.33
- 79.33 – 84.41
- 84.41 – 89.73

Ancient Migration

When people move from one place to another, it is called migration. Humans have been migrating for many thousands of years and many people are still migrating today.

The first human migration was around 60,000 years ago when very early **homo sapiens** began leaving Africa for the first time and migrating to other continents around the world.

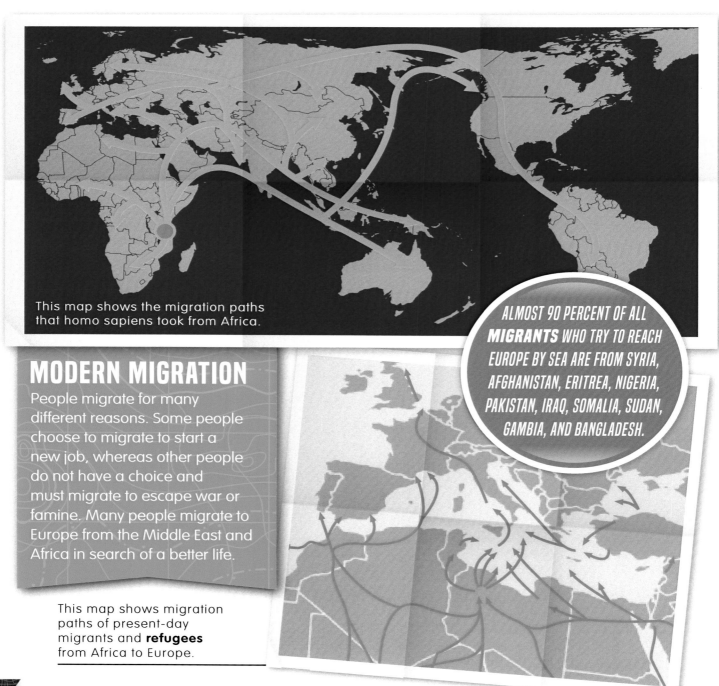

This map shows the migration paths that homo sapiens took from Africa.

MODERN MIGRATION

People migrate for many different reasons. Some people choose to migrate to start a new job, whereas other people do not have a choice and must migrate to escape war or famine. Many people migrate to Europe from the Middle East and Africa in search of a better life.

ALMOST 90 PERCENT OF ALL **MIGRANTS** WHO TRY TO REACH EUROPE BY SEA ARE FROM SYRIA, AFGHANISTAN, ERITREA, NIGERIA, PAKISTAN, IRAQ, SOMALIA, SUDAN, GAMBIA, AND BANGLADESH.

This map shows migration paths of present-day migrants and **refugees** from Africa to Europe.

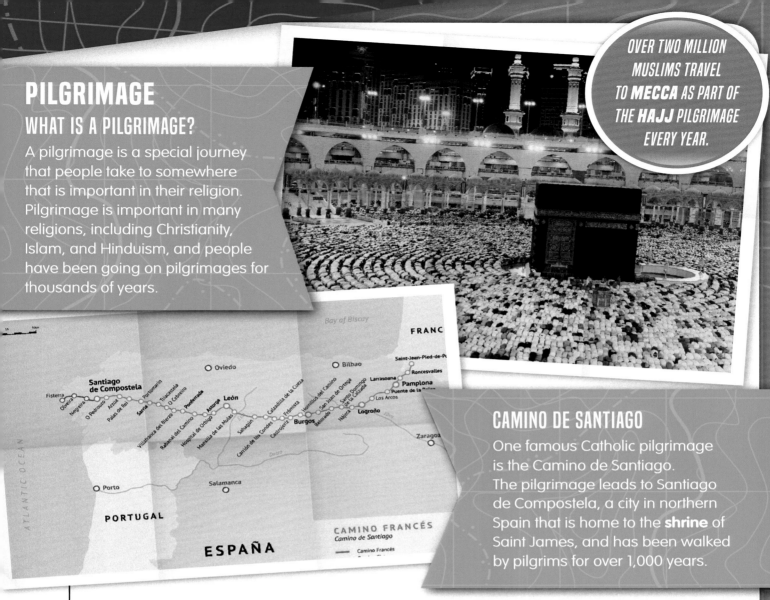

PILGRIMAGE

WHAT IS A PILGRIMAGE?

A pilgrimage is a special journey that people take to somewhere that is important in their religion. Pilgrimage is important in many religions, including Christianity, Islam, and Hinduism, and people have been going on pilgrimages for thousands of years.

OVER TWO MILLION MUSLIMS TRAVEL TO *MECCA* AS PART OF THE *HAJJ* PILGRIMAGE EVERY YEAR.

CAMINO DE SANTIAGO

One famous Catholic pilgrimage is the Camino de Santiago. The pilgrimage leads to Santiago de Compostela, a city in northern Spain that is home to the **shrine** of Saint James, and has been walked by pilgrims for over 1,000 years.

This map shows the route that pilgrims take through France towards Santiago de Compostela.

Andhra Pradesh

Andhra Pradesh is a **state** in India with many Hindu shrines. The shrines are dedicated to the Hindu gods Vishnu, Shiva, and Shakti. Hindu pilgrims travel hundreds of miles to worship at these shrines.

This map shows the shrines in Andhra Pradesh, and the roads that pilgrims may take to travel between the shrines.

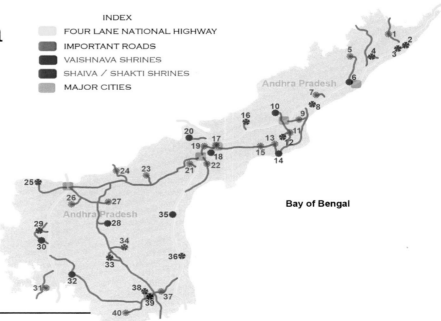

INDEX
- FOUR LANE NATIONAL HIGHWAY
- IMPORTANT ROADS
- VAISHNAVA SHRINES
- SHAIVA / SHAKTI SHRINES
- MAJOR CITIES

MAPPING AND SAFETY

Maps come in many forms. Maps that are useful for driving and finding routes can be found in a large book called an atlas, and some maps of the world are printed as a poster that can be stuck on the wall. Maps can now be found on smartphones and computers, with many people relying on map apps to help them navigate their local area, and even the world.

To travel to most countries, you need a passport and money. For some countries, you even need a **visa**. However, many refugees leave their country very quickly because they are escaping war, and this makes it difficult to have all the correct things. For this reason, many asylum seekers must find their own way, avoiding **border control** and passport checkpoints. Many rely on **GPS** and smartphone apps to help them find directions for a safe journey.

Refugees from Damascus, the capital of Syria, might have to walk as far as 2,700 miles (4,340 km) to get to London.

London

Damascus

RACIAL SEGREGATION

Although slavery was **abolished** in the U.S. in 1865, for a long time afterward black people were still not allowed to use public facilities like schools, restaurants, hairdressers, or hotels. This is called racial segregation, and it carried on for a long time.

During this time, laws called the Jim Crow laws were passed in many southern states of the U.S. They separated black people and white people, and told black people where they could go and what they could do.

The Great Migration

Before the **Civil Rights Act** was introduced in 1964, which gave black people more equality and freedom, around six million black Americans fled to northern and western states to escape the Jim Crow laws of the South. This was called The Great Migration and it began in the early 20th century. Black Americans migrated so that they could feel safe and start a new life.

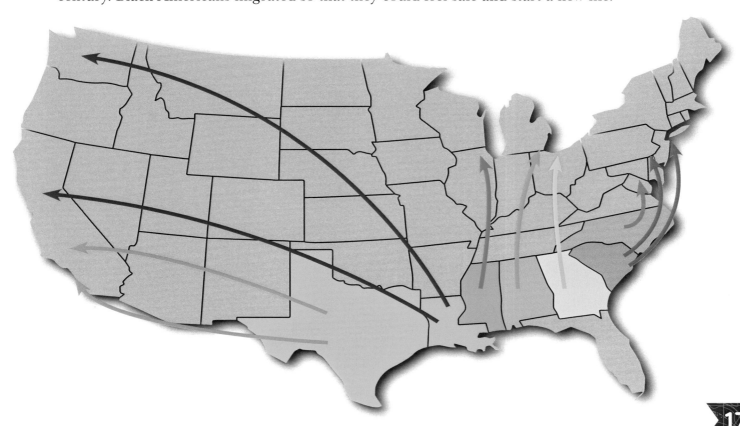

EXPLORERS

The Age of Discovery

During the 15th and 16th centuries, European kings, **merchants**, and explorers were determined to discover new sea routes and new lands. This led to sailors setting out on long and dangerous expeditions across the world and into the unknown. This period in history is often called the Age of Exploration, or the Age of Discovery.

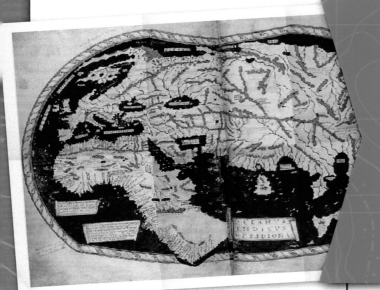

CHRISTOPHER COLUMBUS

Christopher Columbus was an explorer during the Age of Discovery. When he was young, he earned money by making and selling maps with his brother, but his dream was to go to sea.

In 1492, he sailed from Spain to America with three ships and a crew of around 90 men. Their task was to find a new route to China and India by sailing west. However, Columbus never reached Asia. Instead, he landed in the Bahamas and became one of the first Europeans to set foot on these lands.

This is a map made in 1489 by a German man named Heinrich Hammer. Europeans did not know about the Americas yet, so they are not shown on the map.

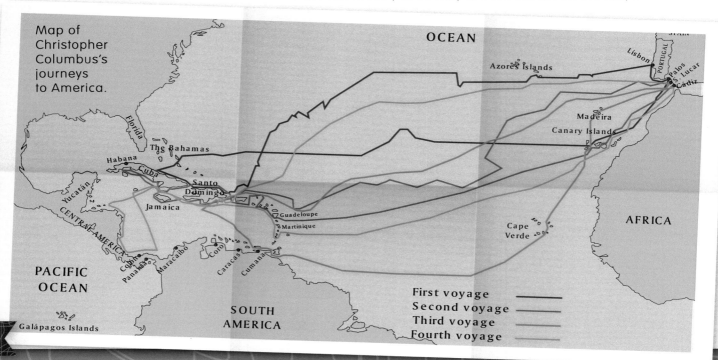

Map of Christopher Columbus's journeys to America.

First voyage _____
Second voyage _____
Third voyage _____
Fourth voyage _____

Captain James Cook

Captain James Cook was an explorer who left England in 1768 for his first voyage to sail towards the South Pacific. Cook traveled around New Zealand and the eastern coast of Australia, places which had not been explored by Europeans before. Cook was a very skilled cartographer and drew maps of these coastlines as he traveled round them. Cook mapped more than 4,970 miles (8,000 km) of coastline that were unknown to Europeans and had never been mapped before. These maps helped future explorers navigate Australia and New Zealand safely.

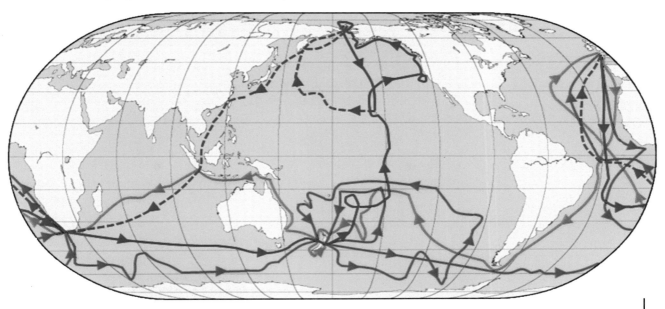

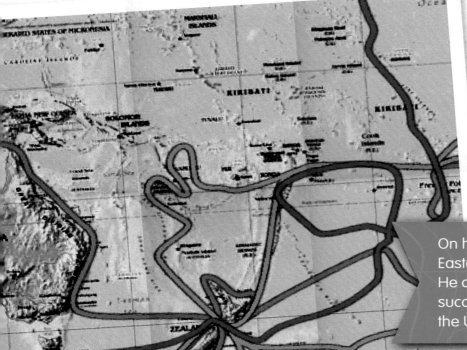

	1st Voyage
	2nd Voyage
	3rd Voyage

These maps show James Cook's voyages to Australia, New Zealand, and the South Pacific islands. During his third voyage, Cook was killed in Hawaii. The dotted line shows his crew's return journey to England.

On his future trips, James Cook traveled to Easter Island, North America, and Hawaii. He continued his work on cartography and successfully mapped the northwest coast of the U.S. as well as Alaska.

SPACE RACE

Eventually, people's appetite for exploration started to look beyond Earth and up into the stars. In the 1960s, the U.S. and the **Soviet Union** began competing with each other to have the most advanced space technology, and to get into space – and especially on the moon – first. This became known as the Space Race, and ended in 1969 when U.S. **NASA** astronauts Neil Armstrong and Buzz Aldrin walked on the moon.

AFTER FOLLOWING A VERY EXACT ROUTE, IT TOOK THE APOLLO 11 SPACECRAFT AROUND THREE DAYS TO REACH THE MOON.

Buzz Aldrin, Neil Armstrong, and Michael Collins were launched into space inside the Apollo 11 spacecraft on July 16, 1969, and returned to Earth eight days later, after traveling somewhere that had never been explored by humans before.

The first human footprint on the moon

While Buzz Aldrin and Neil Armstrong were on the moon, they collected samples of the surface to bring back to Earth. They also took many photos and measurements of the landing site that could be used to create maps for future astronauts and moon walkers.

Moon Walkers

Just as maps are vital in exploring new lands on Earth, mapping the moon became important in space exploration. When people discover a place for the first time, it is important that the explorers draw maps of the area and write down any interesting details about the new place. This helps any future people who may want to travel there. These maps can include geographical features like **craters** or mountains, the paths they took, and where they left any objects behind.

This picture of the moon shows where Apollo 11 landed.

This photo of the Apollo 11 landing site was taken in 2012.

Camera

LM

LRRR

Discarded Cover

PSEP

50 m

Footprints on the moon create a map of where humans have walked.

POLITICAL MAPS: COUNTRIES AND BORDERS

Political Maps

Many of the maps we use in everyday life are political maps. Political maps show the borders of countries, states, and counties, and the locations of towns and cities. Borders and boundaries are decided by humans and often change depending on things like wars between different countries and states. Unfortunately, there are often many wars happening around the world, so political maps are constantly changing.

This is a current political map of North America.

AFRICA

Political maps of Africa have changed a lot throughout history. Areas of Africa have been invaded and **colonized** by Belgium, Germany, Spain, France, Great Britain, Italy, Portugal, and the **Ottoman Empire**. In the late 19th century, European countries drew maps and divided Africa into new countries so that they could distribute the areas between themselves.

This is a map of Africa made in the Middle East in 1803. It shows the areas that the Ottoman Empire recognized as being countries.

Great Britain
Belgium
Germany
Spain
Italy
Portugal
France

This is a European map of Africa in 1913 that shows the African borders created by Europe and the areas that were colonized and ruled by different countries.

EUROPE

ROMAN EMPIRE

Borders in Europe have also changed a lot, and continue to change today. From the year 27 BC until AD 476, the Roman Empire ruled much of Europe and some of the Middle East. The Roman Empire was based in Rome, Italy, but spread all the way to present-day Britain, Portugal, Turkey, and North Africa.

This political map shows the Roman Empire in AD 125 and the countries that existed at the time.

Kingdoms

When the Roman Empire fell in AD 476, many new kingdoms appeared in Europe. These kingdoms were the Frankish kingdom of present-day France and Germany, the Visigothic kingdom of Spain and Portugal, and the Avar kingdom of Eastern Europe. These kingdoms fought each other to rule over the old lands of the Roman Empire.

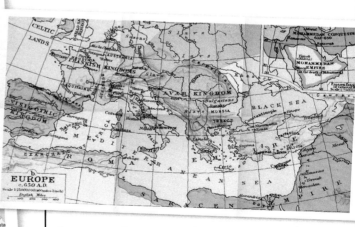

This map of Europe is from AD 650 and shows the areas that each kingdom ruled.

In recent years, these kingdoms have been separated. Various wars have occurred in Europe, including both World Wars, and now the continent has been split into much smaller, individual countries.

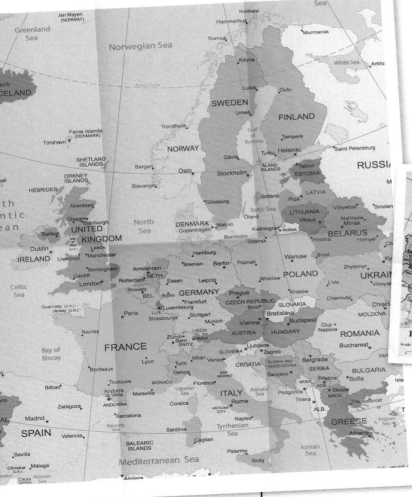

Modern Map of Europe

MAPPING THE SKY

What Is Astronomy?

Astronomy is a type of science that involves studying stars, planets, and anything else that we might be able to see in space. People have been interested in studying space for thousands of years, with the earliest astronomers coming from ancient Mesopotamia, in the Middle East. Astronomers in Mesopotamia studied the stars and created constellations to measure the passing of time and mark the seasons of the year.

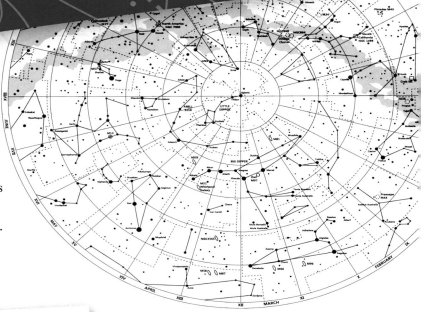

CONSTELLATIONS

Humans do not just map the Earth; they also map the sky by creating and naming constellations. Constellations are groups of stars that make a particular shape in the night sky. Many constellations were discovered hundreds or thousands of years ago and have special names. People have been mapping constellations for many hundreds, even thousands, of years to help people identify and track different areas of the sky, and to help with navigation.

THE NORTH STAR, OR POLARIS, IS FOUND IN THE URSA MINOR, OR LITTLE DIPPER, CONSTELLATION AND IS DIRECTLY ABOVE THE NORTH POLE.

Constellation maps are maps of the sky that can help people navigate and find the direction of north, south, east, and west.

HEAD NORTH

Before compasses, GPS, or topographical maps, many people relied on the sun, moon, and stars to help them find their way around the world. This is called celestial navigation. The North Star is very important for celestial navigation because it remains in the same place in the sky while all the other stars appear to rotate around it. If someone can find the North Star and draw an imaginary line down to the **horizon**, it will show them which direction north is.

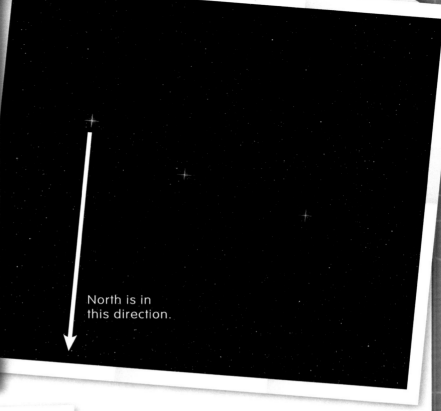

North is in this direction.

Constellations can also teach us a lot about the ancient civilizations that first drew them. There are 88 different constellations in the sky and 48 of these were mapped in ancient Greece.

One of the most recognized constellations is Orion, a figure in Greek mythology. He traditionally appears in Greek myths as an archer or a hunter, but Orion and his constellation also feature in other cultures around the world, including Egypt, Hungary, and Scandinavia.

These three stars are called Orion's Belt.

GOOGLE EARTH

Navigation

With the growth and development of satellite navigation technology, also called satnav, people no longer have to rely on stars to find their way. One popular satnav website and app is Google Maps, which features a map of the whole world and allows people to plan routes and journeys to almost any location. Google Maps gives directions based on whether you want to drive, walk, cycle, take public transportation, or take an airplane.

Google Street View Car

GOOGLE NOW USES CAMERAS FITTED TO BACKPACKS AND SNOWMOBILES TO COLLECT IMAGES FROM PLACES WHERE THEY CANNOT TAKE CARS.

STREET VIEW

Street View on Google Maps is a new way of mapping the world. Special cars and tricycles are fitted with 360° cameras before being sent on various routes to take photographs. The photos are all put together to create panoramic views of many streets and cities on Earth.

- Full Coverage
- Some Coverage
- Full/Some Coverage Planned
- Views of Select Business/ Tourist Attractions
- Views of Private Businesses
- No Coverage

This map shows how much of each country is available to see on Google Street View.

GEOGUESSR

GEOGUESSR

Many games have been released that use Google Street View. One of these games is Geoguessr, which involves being dropped somewhere in the world on Google Street View. The aim of the game is to guess where you are by exploring the area and looking for clues like landmarks, street signs, or people.

Google Forest

As part of their mapping software, Google collects satellite images of Earth taken from the sky. These images are brought together to create a giant map of the world in the form of a globe, called Google Earth. By zooming in to view the Earth more closely, Google Earth allows you to explore different countries and areas in detail.

In 2005, **botanists** from Kew Gardens, London, used Google Earth to try to find new areas to explore in Africa. They soon discovered a rain forest on Mount Mabu in Mozambique that had never been seen by scientists before. The rain forest now has the nickname "Google Forest."

Mount Mabu

MAPPING FOR FUN

Pokémon GO

Pokémon GO is a smartphone game that was released in 2016. The game uses the smartphone's GPS location to place the player's avatar onto a Pokémon version of a map of the surrounding area. Players move their avatar around the game's map by moving around their real-world surroundings. By following the game's map and visiting real-life locations like a local landmark or a nearby shop, players can catch Pokémon or visit "Pokéstops" that appear on the screen.

Pokémon GO relies on GPS location services and online mapping software.

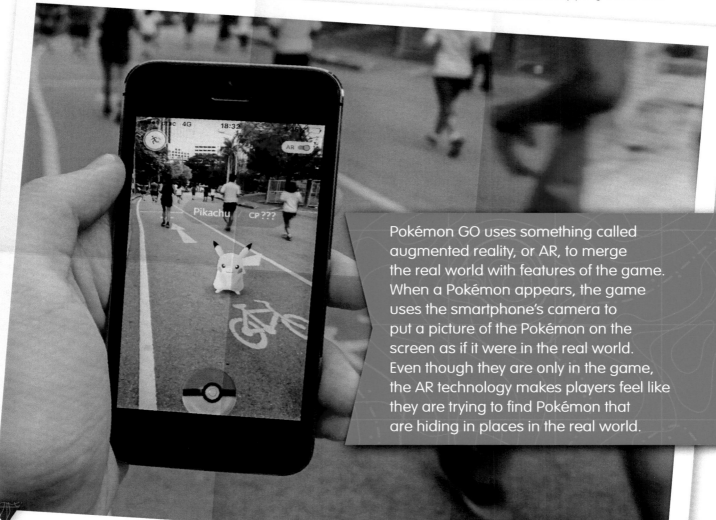

Pokémon GO uses something called augmented reality, or AR, to merge the real world with features of the game. When a Pokémon appears, the game uses the smartphone's camera to put a picture of the Pokémon on the screen as if it were in the real world. Even though they are only in the game, the AR technology makes players feel like they are trying to find Pokémon that are hiding in places in the real world.

GEOCACHING

Like Pokémon Go, Geocaching also uses GPS technology. However, rather than using it as part of an augmented reality game, Geocaching uses GPS as a real-world treasure-hunting game. Geocaching involves following a set of **coordinates** to find hidden geocaches.

GPS Device

How Do You Find a Geocache?

Geocaches are the treasure chests you are hunting for. A geocache is usually a small container that has a logbook and a few small objects inside. To find a geocache, you must first register to become a member of Geocaching. After this, you can search for your zip code on the Geocaching website and see if there are any hidden geocaches nearby. Once you have found a geocache on the website, you can input the coordinates into some mapping software on a smartphone or a GPS device. This will give you directions to the geocache. Many geocachers sign the logbook and swap an object in the geocache with something they have brought with them.

Geocache

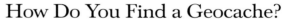

TRAP STREETS

Cartographers, or mapmakers, spend a lot of time researching and preparing each map. Before satellites, when maps had to be **chartered** and drawn by hand, it was important for cartographers to protect their work from thieves who might want to copy it. Mapmakers would do this by including trap streets in their maps. Trap streets are fake roads, towns, or other details that do not really exist but are deliberately included in a map. If someone did steal a company's map and pretend it was theirs, they would be discovered by the trap street.

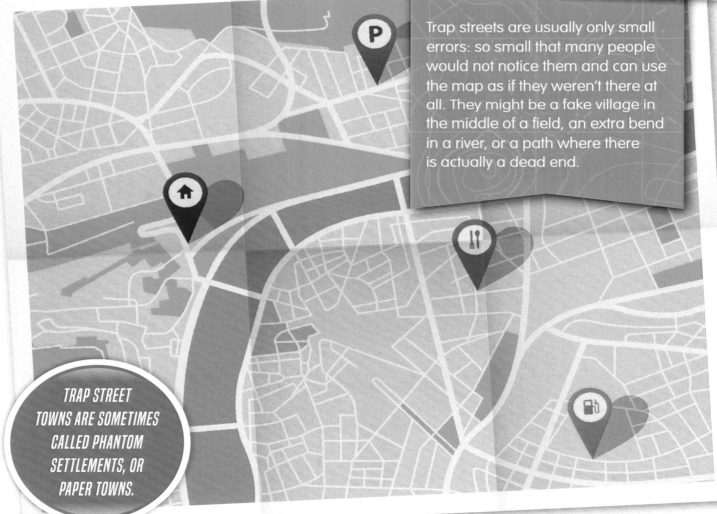

Trap streets are usually only small errors: so small that many people would not notice them and can use the map as if they weren't there at all. They might be a fake village in the middle of a field, an extra bend in a river, or a path where there is actually a dead end.

TRAP STREET TOWNS ARE SOMETIMES CALLED PHANTOM SETTLEMENTS, OR PAPER TOWNS.

abolished	to get rid of or do away with something, especially laws
border control	points on the borders between countries where migrants are checked
botanists	scientists who study plant life
chartered	officially ordered to produce something
Civil Rights Act	a set of laws in the U.S. thatt protect people's civil rights, especially the right to equality
colonized	when people from one country go and take over another to live there
color coded	when different colors are used to represent different information
coordinates	points where a vertical and horizontal line meet on a map that are used for finding out the location of something
craters	hollow, bowl-shaped areas, for example on the surface of the moon
diagrams	simplified drawings that show the appearance, structure, or workings of something
distribution	how things are shared
diversity	having a variety
drought	a long period of very little rainfall, which leads to a lack of water
famine	when large numbers of people have little or no food
features	distinctive properties of the landscape
GPS	Global Positioning System: public system of satellites for determining position on Earth
hajj	the pilgrimage to Mecca that every Muslim is expected to make at least once
homo sapiens	the scientific name for human beings
horizon	the line where the Earth and sky seem to meet
landmarks	parts of the landscape that can be used as reference points
Mecca	the religious capital of Saudi Arabia and the Muslim world
merchants	people who buy and sell goods to make a profit
migrants	people who move from one country to another to settle and live
NASA	National Aeronautics and Space Administration: the U.S. organization that conducts space travel and research
navigation	finding your way or planning directions
Ottoman Empire	Turkish empire lasting from 1300 to 1918
refugees	people forced to migrate by terrible circumstances, e.g., war, famine, or natural disaster
shrines	sacred places or objects dedicated to a holy person or god
Soviet Union	a country made up of fifteen republics in Eastern Europe, including Russia, which was separated in 1991
state	an area of land or population governed by a single government
statisticians	people whose profession is working with statistics and data
territory	a particular area of land belonging to a country
topographical	showing the shape of the Earth's surface
visa	permission granted to allow someone to travel or work in a particular country

INDEX